The Macabre Masterpiece: Poems of Horror and Gore

Justin Bienvenue

The Macabre Masterpiece: Poems of Horror and Gore

Copyright 2013 by Justin Bienvenue

All rights reserved. This book is a reproduction transmitted in a form fit to the authors original intent and in no way may be reproduced in or by any other form without the written permission of the author.

All poems within the book were thought of and written by the author and no one else. Any resemblance or likeness to any person living or dead, event or place is entirely coincidental.

Authors Website:
http://jbienvenue.webs.com/

The Operating Table of Contents
Chapter 1: Hell
Buried Alive
Depths of Hell
The Minions
The Rage of Burning Envy
The Grim Reaper
They Without Morals
Rage of Hades
Declaration of Decadence
Hell's Guardian
Summoners of the Unholy

Chapter 2: Blood
Blood
The River of Blood
The River of Blood pt.2
The River of Blood pt.3
Tears of Blood
Tears of Blood pt.2
The Massacre
The Screaming of Bloody Murder
Bloodstorm
Slaughterhouse

Chapter 3: Creatures
Vampires
Vampires pt.2
Vampires pt.3
Vampires pt.4
Dracul
Zombies

Werewolves
Frankenstein
The Untamed Beast
Gargoyles
Chapter 4: Creepy
The Black
Dark V. Light
The Legend of the Ship on Mystery Pier
Sounds of the Season
The Fever
Solitary
The Dead
The Portrait of Dorian Gray
Labinnac Forest
Sinister Endeavors
Chapter 5: Suspense
Chambers of Fire
Collector of Bones
Wager of Death
The Nightwatchman
Thirteen Stairs
Death Labyrinth
Resurrection
The Philosophy of Carnage
Inhibitors of Doom
The Executioner

"Deep into that darkness peering, long I stood there, wondering, fearing, doubting, dreaming dreams no mortal ever dared to dream before" -Edgar Allan Poe

The Macabre Masterpiece: Poems of Horror and Gore

Chapter 1: Hell

Buried Alive

Six fit under is where you should be
Buried deep in the cemetery
Under the ground confined in a casket
Better that then your head not chopped into a basket
Properly given a solid tombstone
Dead in the earth from vein to bone
Rotting, decaying, slowly losing form
Your corpse is getting cold far from warm
I hope you enjoy your eternal resting place
And I can just imagine the look on your face
Should be calm and peaceful, no need to thrive
But then again you were buried alive..

Depths of Hell

Burning through the depths of hell
Running around as I scream and yell
Engulfed in flames I'm about to melt away
Pretty soon I'll have nothing to say
The lava is flowing and it's scorching hot
Here in hell as I rot
Half of my face is no more
It was burned down to the core
Floating in the lava I can see coal
Soon the devil will acquire my soul
With just minutes to live I think of all I've learned
But it doesn't matter anymore for I'm brittle and burned

The Minions

Wreaking of havoc, mayhem and breath
Out comes the disciples of carnage and death
The minions who make the brimstone burn
Put your intestines on a crane as they slowly begin to turn
Defy all that's holy, for they are the seekers
Do the bidding for they are the devil's speakers
They carry a burden and drag a heavy boulder
Around hot surroundings, their insides are colder
Their faces disfigured, charred and melted
From all the pain they have ever dealt with
A lonesome look about them perhaps sadness
This being for who they work for derived of complete madness
Their job is never done and it never will be
Working off the sins for all eternity

The Rage of Burning Envy

Judgements flames burn all who dare
Apocalyptic destruction lit like a flare
Meltdown, mayhem, malice and mace
Your soul indeed did the devil enjoy to taste
Too hot to tell how tales from beyond
The fire filled grounds continued to carry on
Victims wailing and screaming in pain
Some have for so long they are now insane
Punished are the ones who look down on fate
And now the future awaits with the opening of Hell's Gate
With all the workers he has the devil can never have too many
As he welcomes all with the rage of burning envy

The Grim Reaper

The spirit of the dead is near
They've asked me to bring you all here
I can see it in your eyes
You all look despaired
I'd like to help you but I no longer care
I no longer can
It's ripping my insides out and nothings there
I'm a victim to my own domain
To which I've put myself in my own pain
That's why they have chosen me
They know I'll bring them victory
My wrist have never bled
But you can still see some red
They have now closed the cage
I'm in a bit of rage
But there's nothing I can do
Because people helping me is through
Some will never ever get to know me in person
Cause now I'm all alone in this Ancient Dungeon

They Without Morals

Who dares disturb those who sleep in deep slumber?
Deriving us from our caskets and tombs
Whoever you are it is but a wonder
And onto you I curse and cast doom
You have ruined our peace and tainted our dirt
Do you have not any shame?
For this I summon onto you the deadliest hurt
And inflict blasphemy to scorn your name
Now let's see you get into heaven
Knowing you've angered those already there
I plague you with the deadly sins of seven
Until your distraught and can no longer bare
A cemetery is a confined place for the dead
You did not come to pay your respects
For every step in which your feet have tread
You shall feel the mortifying effects

Rage of Hades

I'm brutally defacing anyone in my path
My agenda is quite simple to cause chaos and wrath
My explanation for this? Well there isn't one
This just happens to be my definition of fun
Words I go by; onslaught, mayhem, carnage and destruction
Without these four things surely I could not function
My plan of action is to cause total devastation
Until I cause havoc and there's complete humiliation
Chemical warfare if you will because I'm chemically imbalanced
Putting people in early graves is just one of my many talents
Why kill two birds with one stone? I go for the whole nest
I am not satisfied with my work unless someone's a bloody mess
Until the look on their faces has them mortally mortified
Their next stop should be the morgue but their gonna be buried alive
There is no caution just consequence you've been warned
If you defy this simple task you'll be wishing you were never born

Declaration of Decadence

We hold no truths here and nothing is evident
No soul is treated equal this is no sacrament
Those that are here rot, they are not endowed by their creator
They are alienable, have no rights and the devil is their savior
There is no life without death, liberty without tyranny
And the pursuit of happiness here is just irony
You need no consent cause here your just a slave
Your body on earth decaying in it's grave
Let this stand as your only rights given
You don't deserve any since your no longer living
This goes way beyond any sacred document
Consider it to be your final event
When you lived you went by independence
Here you believe in the Declaration of Decadence

Hell's Guardian

He stands by the gates with a hammer and shield
Those who wish to pass must first yield
He must look you over from head to toe
To truly make sure this is where you are to go
The underworld is taken quite seriously
And no one besides the devil is more inferior then he
Don't get me wrong hell takes anyone
But those beyond pure of the heart are shun
And it's his job to bring forth judgement
Consider him the advisor of hell's budget
He looks for those with the darkest of souls
Or those who look easy to control
From lost spirits and brimstone he was created
Challenge him and prepare to be annihilated
However there is a price at fighting so hard
If you beat him there will be a changing of the guard

Summoners of the Unholy

Off in the distance chants can be heard
Conjuring up beings from the written word
From bats to demons to grotesque monsters
They are the real things, far from impostors
They speak in the form of the ancient tongue
Casting their words deep from the lungs
It's hard to understand what's being said
Unless you understand the Tibetan Book of the Dead
This is the text in which the strange spells derive
The innocent better run if they wish to stay alive
Soon a whole army of terror will be present
Things are about to be vile instead of pleasant
Is there anyone that dares to act boldly?
And put a stop to the summoners of the unholy

Chapter 2: Blood

Blood

Flowing down like a stream
It sickens and stains it's no dream
Having none would make you dead
Even when you have some and it rushes to your head
It leaks out and you loose life
From a cut which was given by a knife
Abundant amounts of it intensify the pain
Dripping down like drops of rain
It's the liquid that vampires drain
Leaving you weak and plain
No matter what we always dread
It's the true meaning in the color of red

The River of Blood

Let the red run slowly into the stream
In this river your hands will not be washed clean
Guilt will arise and your skin will stain
Plain and drained to the vein from those you've slain
Nor will it be cleansed even after the first rain
It eats at your brain contains bane until you go insane
Consumed and overwhelmed with tears of hate
A slate far from great earns a trip straight to Hell's Gate
Directed by doom you sealed your own fate
To anticipate or wait with no mind state or heart rate
The stream overflows causing a flood
Wash thy hands in the river of blood

The River of Blood pt.2

It's still flowing and as colorful as ever
Pumping in more water from the touch of a lever
The color is as it always has been a thickly settled red
With bodies constantly drifting ashore dead
So many hands have been cleansed and washed here
So many victims have been taken and disappear
In most bodies of water your reflection can be seen
However not in this one, but you may see someone's spleen
Floating along like it's an everyday sight
Well at least here it is no matter day or night
Going fishing here isn't something you wish
And most likely you'll find a lot more than fish
Here comes another storm to cause a massive flood
And overflowing and destroying is the river of blood

The River of Blood pt.3

It's time once again for the annual flood
And for thou to wash thy hands in the river of blood
You know the red flowing stream that brings out your fears
Causes hysteria, hallucinations, tears and nightmares
Yeah that river, number one blood supplier and storage
Turning the skin red, the mind a clockwork orange
Can't swim in this river I mean you can If you want to
But most likely the blood of those in there will haunt you
We all know that between blood and water bloods thicker
This perhaps means that in this river you die quicker
But who am I to judge? Your just washing your hands
Unless of course what else is in there has other plans
Maybe it's easier to clean when only covered in mud
But then again this is the river of blood

Tears of Blood

With anguish no thoughts and traits of despair
The shadows of sadness fill and plague the air
An unsettling feeling which cannot be escaped
As darkness takes over like a curtain which has been draped
No need to run and waste ones energy
Whatever is expected is not what's expected to be
The taste of ash and smell of burning embers
Takes over and consumes until you can no longer remember
Why you feared what you feared in the first place
Time is now still no feelings of being chased
Just calmness and utter confusion
In the distance a figure, is it an illusion?
Suddenly it presents itself and you soon feel a flood
You've been scared out of your mind and now cry tears of blood

Tears of Blood pt.2

It made itself known to an unlucky soul
It crept and lingered until in control
Out of the black it fed off the fear
Because the person had no clue it was near
With it's job done and one victim gone
It continues to carry on and on
Until it finds yet another
Innocent to feed on and discover
Just like the first the rest will have no clue
And when they see it will know not what to do
Then to just stand there and collapse in horror
And end up on an episode of Law and Order
A body dropped and made only a thud
Last thing shed were tears of blood

The Massacre

No trace of a pulse, heartbeat or breathing
Just a black mark, blood stains and stench of wreaking
Deep cuts, small cuts, in the skin seeping
Injuries on the inside were slowly creeping
Inflicting such a pain that it went onto the outside
This body went through a very gruesome ride
The wounds are major anything but slightly
A slowly painless death seems highly unlikely
More like the opposite in fact possibly horrendous
Massive blood loss, sheared liver, kidneys and appendix
Whatever did this knew all the right places
Did I forget to mention it left our victim here faceless?
One can only imagine if this person dared to cough
With such deep lacerations and fingertips burned off
Indeed they went through the worst misery
But as to who they are is a total mystery

The Screaming of Bloody Murder

Guests socialize in a ballroom conversing in chatter
A door slams abruptly with vigorous force
They soon all rush to the room too see what's the matter
Looking around trying to find the source
They look down before them to find the unexpected
A body lays dead on the floor
No trace of anyone else or a weapon is detected
Just a puddle and presence of gore
They talk amongst themselves clearly shaken
Everything seemed so calm
They wonder if another life will be taken
And who would want to inflict harm
Soon there's another startling noise
The killing has traveled further
Everyone begins to loose their poise
Upon the cries and screaming of bloody murder

Bloodstorm

The sky turns scarlet as red clouds fill the air
About to cause a disaster that no one can repair
Rain begins to fall but people soon begin to dread
Because they soon realize that the rain is in fact red
Soon it begins to hail large baseball sized blood rocks
With enough in them to put a shame to blood clots
Lakes, rivers and waterfalls soon become tainted
Everything now covered looking like it's been painted
Those outside are now completely drenched
Unless you're a vampire then your thirst has been quenched
The rain continues to pore, such a horrifying display
Weathermen were wrong it's not a sunny day
The sky now scorched with everything in distortion
A storm for the ages in epic proportion

Slaughterhouse

Up on a hill sits an old stingy place
Where it looks abandoned but hasn't gone to waste
Take a step inside and witness the filthy horror
Enough to make one sick and tarnish ones aura
Corpses and carcasses lay dead on the floor
Blood stains everywhere surrounded by gore
The need for bloodshed is done in the back of the shed
In the back of the head until the back is red
All around are axes, machetes, butcher knifes and saws
Body parts of gutted people and animals desecrated and raw
Destroyed and mutilated beyond recognition
What and whoever did this made it their mission
Walls, doors and windows no longer clean
Dirty and disturbed no longer sheen
With all that's here you could collect blood by the ounce
Wipe off your feet before entering the slaughterhouse

Chapter 3: Creatures

Vampires

They lurk and feast in the night
In a view that's out of site
Creeping, watching as you walk
All they do is prey and stalk
As piercing as a ravens peck
As their fangs dig into your neck
Drinking your blood so they can be stronger
For another 1000 years they can live longer
One way to kill them is to stab them with a stake
Or push them in the sunlight and watch them bake
A holy cross burns them with fear
Yelling and giving a horrifying sneer
You try and try to put up a fight
For they are the creatures of the night

Vampires pt.2

Back again to tell the tale
About the dark and the pale
Still bringing the fright and the terror
Since the days of the Victorian Era
They who live without consequence
Their lives for years full of suspense
Their complexion so gaunt yet so pure
Such strong attraction of loom and allure
Captivating is their radiant physique
So soft and charming when they speak
They don't always try to cause a fray
At some point they look for a protege
One who will continue on the great legacy
To give one a feeling of truly feeling free
They can go into seclusion, perish but never retire
Once you become one your forever a vampire

Vampires pt.3

The nights are endless but for them time stands still
As it always has been along with the lust to kill
One must wonder how living so long can be
There's certainly more to it then just feeling free
Through the years it must take its toll
To contain control without a reflection or soul
Perhaps for some the days grow longer
Wondering if the thought of death does ponder
To just step into the light and throw it all away
But then restless they roam the spirit must stay
So ironically in death still not completely at peace
A legend with unfinished business wishing to be deceased
On the earth for centuries walking around undead
Now finally getting rest only to walk around again

Vampires pt.4

Still roaming the earth after all this time
But then again immortality is not a crime
The search for another these days isn't as easy
And when one is found they get and feel queasy
For them the past has never been erasable
Their lust for blood still and forever insatiable
By now those still living are elders and walking myths
Still giving mortals their unbelievable gifts
Some so strong now it takes longer to be harmed by fire
Always with that essence and spark of desire
Another century in which they patiently embark
But always confined and hidden in the dark
If they were to die now it would be by their own hand
No one hunts anymore and it's life they can't stand
But then again these are just words so who am I to say?
The creatures of the night in which Vlad has paved the way

Dracul

He is the vapor, the air, the monster, the essence
He does not have to be close for you to feel his presence
The blood that runs through him is not his own
He takes any form in which he wants to be known
His story has been told throughout the ages
Changed over time and appears on many pages
He does not lust like the rest he loves what he's lost
Who he is now is due to being double crossed
He hides away and at times walks around like normal
He is the one, the definition of immortal
The Leader, the count, the general, the creator
Prince of Darkness, Dracula, Vlad the Impaler

<u>Zombies</u>

Out of the graveyard they begin to rise
Small, medium, large in every size
Pale like appearance, pasty complexion
They are dead and do not offer affection
Their walk is slow yet they still bring fear
It takes forever for them to be near
If they do get you they'll use cannibal tactics
Cause when it comes to body parts they are addicts
Sometimes all it takes for them is one cough
And boom an arm or a leg falls off
It's something creepy indeed to dread
So watch out for Uh! The dawn of the dead

Werewolves

When a full moon comes out so does this story
About a creature whose tactics are beyond gory
Howls can be heard from miles away
And at night they arise to come out and play
Lurking and looking for a tasty treat
It senses heat and is craving some meat
It's fangs as sharp as a kitchen knife
Hunting down people taking life after life
Don't be frightened they can smell when your scared
They can catch you off guard when your least prepared
What was once a man is now no more
Not just clothes but skin tissue also tore
And tearing things to pieces is what it loves to do
So be very careful or the werewolves will find you

Frankenstein

He is perhaps the most horrendous creation
Made for whatever means but certainly not salvation
On a night where a mighty storm turned into a great event
Down in a creepy basement began this experiment
A doctor gone mad makes what ends up a disaster
Assisted by a small ugly man who calls him master
He begins the procedure by making incisions
Propping what's on the table in a rigorous position
He attaches conductors that will transmit the volts
So on both sides go the big wide bolts
Suddenly lightning strikes and the creature thrives
The doctor laughs evilly and screams IT'S ALIVE!
The experiment a success, he proclaims it to be divine
For he has created a being, the monster of Frankenstein

The Untamed Beast

An untamed beast looks to unleash his fury
Sending all those around him in a state of worry
They begin to panic and then start to run
Not truly realizing what they've just done
They have given the beast a reason to kill
He sees sudden movement which triggers a thrill
With his instincts alert he soon attacks
Taking out everyone in his tracks
He slashes and shreds and tears through skin
Till he gets to the bones brittle and thin
He chews on the bones with his teeth so keen
And with his slimy tongue licks them clean
He looks around and his eyes begin to widen
He finds more people that have been hidin'
He smells their flesh and snarls with a roar
Jumping into the air he begins to soar
He lands on top of them and begins his onslaught
Gripping and ripping and ripping them apart
He lets out a yell to show he's enjoyed his feast
Just another tasty dinner for the untamed beast

Gargoyles

Crouching in position posing in perfect posture
On the rooftop of a gothic cathedral sits a monster
He overlooks the city with an amazing aerial view
Contemplating on exactly what to do
With the sky now at twilight he slowly begins to move
Sneaky, sly and ever so smooth
He spreads his wings and lets out a fierce growl
As his eyes light up more alerting then an owl
Jumps off the building and into the air he soars
Viewing the nightlife and victims as he explores
He lurks around and preys on the unexpected
Despite his stature and size he remains undetected
After he's done feasting and adventuring about
He heads back to the church so no one figures him out
Back into his spot as a statue so his image does not spoil
Now just a stone figurine sits the gargoyle

Chapter 4: Creepy

The Black

They're the reason that shadows exist
They're even in the mist
It's the reason we're afraid to go to bed at night
Because there's no light, we're in a fright
Related to evil when personified
Can be deadly when on a ride
Sometimes used as a characteristic
Some believe it to be optimistic
Perhaps it's never really the right track
But also referred to as the black

Dark V. Light

One never knows what lurks deep in the dark
Because the light is too hidden to inflict a spark
Always gloomy in a black mass area
A feeling sets in of loneliness and hysteria
To find light the darkness must be entered
All the way at the end glowing and centered
But it's a long way down and deep within
In order to reach the end you must first begin
Keeping calm preparing for the unknown
It looks easy because the light at times is shown
Into the tunnel continuing on
You reach the end but the light is now gone....

The Legend of the Ship on Mystery Pier

Along the dock of a port town in the mist
Where the population is few but the people do exist
Where the fog clouds the skies and the seas can't be seen
Not a trace of blue in the air just a smoke like green
A ship makes its way as it embarks on it's mission
Makes a pit-stop at this city but it's probably not for fishin'
They get off the ship and head towards town
Not a trace of a crowd or single person around
That's cause all are in their houses looking out their windows
Checking out these grungy guys with weird scruffy clothes
They scrounger up some rum along the port and torch the rest
Then head deeper into the city looking to cause some death
But when brave men come out their homes to try and banish
The other men are gone and seem to vanish
Left behind are burning barrels of rum with no trace of men anywhere
And so goes the legend of the ship on mystery pier

Sounds of the Season

The creaking of boards heard so discrete
The quiet pattering and stomping of feet
Whispers of the wind ruffle against the shutters
Voices can be heard in soft mumbling and stutters
At night the animals screech, chirp and howl
Such volume so pierce, sharp and foul
Eerie music carries and fills every room
Lightning strikes upon a thunderous boom
The wind now whistles into the air
Squeaking sounds made by a rocking chair
Water boiling making a bubbly wave
Grunts and screams over by the grave
For everything we hear there is a reason
In this case we hear the sounds of the season

The Fever

The fever has spread across the town
Leaving all in the grasp of doom
It will all be over soon
And the next step will be down

It expands it's sickness into the crowded street
Hysteria soon sets in after
Consuming everyone it can capture
The deadly process is almost complete

It thrives off the frail and the weak
Coughing only pollutes the air
Just when things seem all but fair
Out of no where it begins to sneak

After it's done it damages onto another
Place with mass population
To wipe out a whole civilization
To which no one will ever recover

Solitary

Locked deep away behind the prison walls
Where no one bothers to visit or make calls
Is a man with shackles and a cold tortured soul
It takes about 12 guards just to have control
Out of all the inmates here he's treated the most
No this ain't Michael Myers this man is more boast
He can actually talk and when he does it's creepy
Screaming during the night he's hardly ever sleepy
Those who have been in long usually show respect
But this man has none or none to detect
The man is indeed exactly of what there is to represent
Of crazed individuals confined by imprisonment

The Dead

A fancy name for the deceased
A better way to put it to say the least
Skin hardly, bones partly
Underground all the dead party
For what? Why their day is nearing
The day of the dead, the fearing
The reeking of flesh which makes your stomach turn
They smell even worse when some of them burn
This is indeed a disgusting site and smell
But hey this is the only way into hell
Is to have such a figure that is so gross
Not to some but probably to most
The white and pale with no more remorse
Now just a sinner, a dead ghostly corpse

The Portrait of Dorian Gray

Here we see a well-mannered handsome man
Who to keep his good looks will do whatever he can
So he agrees for an artist to paint his portrait
Where he shall remain as is but the picture morbid
From then on in his beauty will not fade
His appearance in reality a hidden masquerade
Soon he commits to debauchery and sin
Thinking that against time he will always win
He shuns away his love with arrogance and rejection
As she poisons herself he makes lust his selection
He looks over his portrait which is now grotesque
Mad with rage he stabs the artist to death
He blames him for all his hideous acts
But his soul blackened no longer in tact
He then takes the knife and stabs his painting
To get away from his life he tries escaping
His servants hear a scream and to the room they swarm
they find an aged, withered, horrid man
Beside him the portrait back to it's original form

Labinnac Forest

Just off in the distance of a highway deep in the woods
Sits a quiet little town that's got the goods
A quick short cut and you'll be right on track
Only problem is those who take it don't come back
See the people here are what you'd call "unique"
Keep to themselves acting bizarre and bleak
However, when they see a stranger in their parts roam
They welcome them and make them feel right at home
Asking you the basics where your from, are you okay?
Offering you food and shelter in a nice but eerie way
If you've seen the movies then you would question this
But when in such a situation think nothing is amiss
Your just tired and need to rest for a while
But truly don't know of these peoples ways or style
They take you to the gathering a place of venue
But when you notice their expression you realize you're the menu
If only you read the sign you'd know you were in for a treat
Welcome to Labinnac Forest and Bon appetit

Sinister Endeavors

Sinister ways are the methods of the wicked
Not all good we witness is as its depicted
It's merely a mirage to hide the ominous
What seems so innocent may not be that obvious
Evil can take on many different personas
And no matter what it is, it always seems to know us
Calling out and haunting us like we're the outcasts
Trying to take us over to make sure we don't last
The most evil of all are the odd and the unknown
Those who get in your head without being shown
If they scare you to death then they have succeeded
Or drive you so mad that they're no longer needed
Evil never backs down or surrenders
Until it has reached all of its endeavors

Chapter 5: Suspense

Chambers of Fire

Echoes carry throughout the empty entrance way
Smears of blood stain upon the walls of gray
The corridor lit up every five feet by a torch
Burning swiftly and calmly with a scorch
Off in the distance a white mist appears
The further you walk the closer it nears
It soon goes away as fast as it came
From every direction bursts flame after flame
The entity returns but your unaware
Your too busy getting lit up like a flare
The more you fight the hotter the flames get
Intensifying the burning increasing the sweat
You manage to escape but at the end of the hall
Notice that its not over at all
Up ahead more flames wild with desire
There is no escape from the chambers of fire

Collector of Bones

It's only a saying to have skeletons in the closet
But to one man its true and clearly he's lost it
Open up his closet and what do we find?
Someone who has a very disturbed mind
We see the remains of the human anatomy
Usually we find this many bones in a catastrophe
In a heaping pile sits vertebrae and ribs
Crushed up pieces of tibs and fibs
A whole row of skulls sits on a shelf of their own
Perfectly aligned and white in tone
Why does a psycho keep bones clean?
Then again what does any of it really mean?
It could mean nothing he's just strange and sick
Or maybe he had a bone to pick

Wager of Death

A compulsive gambler decides to make a very big bet
One he nor anyone else would ever forget
With everything ready laid out and set
The man sits down to play a game of Russian Roulette
He has days but this will top them all
He will either walk away or have the ultimate fall
At the table he sits with four odd looking guys
They all look at him with glaring evil eyes
The first two men take their turns, they stay alive
The other two are next they also survive
Finally the gambler pulls the gun to his head
It goes off and he falls to the floor dead
The men vanish as they laugh under their breath
As the gambler paid the price for making a wager of death

The Nightwatchman

A vicious storm rushes in on a cold gloomy night
Joining forces with the darkness all around
Off in the distance a lighthouse, the only trace of light
Rapidly the rain falls into the waters and the ground
No one dares adventure out into the terrorizing tempest
Except a man along the watchtower looking upon the rest

He seems without concern looking out into the sea
As the waves and gales pick up momentum
Unmoved and unimpressed seemingly is he
This courageous mysterious phantom
The storm is getting worse upon every abrupt strike
Lurking over it is this man showing a taste of dislike

The sky sparks as thunder booms and lightning crashes
With ripples ripping against the port-side and shore
The monstrous wind slashes and dashes
Trying to make all that dare defy it no more
Suddenly all at once, all that's happened does at the same time
The lightning, winds, thunder and waves come together in rhyme

The man goes inside and turns the light on at full blast
Casting a bright burst into the black abyss sky
The storm soon becomes calm and no longer vast
And the man says Poseidon you gave it a good try
At pace and peaceful the storm is now all but gone
As the man watches over as the night carries on

Thirteen Stairs

Thirteen stairs each different and unique
The 1st stair starts with a simple creek
The 2nd stair makes one feel chill and bleak
The 3rd stair a switch that makes the lights flick
The 4th stair extreme cold get your feet off it quick!
The 5th stair extreme heat enough to make one sick
The 6th stair gives the body a sudden electric shock
The 7th stair sounds the ticking of the clock
The 8th stair breaks into two no longer one solid block
The 9th stair causes a sneezing attack
The 10th stair is merely coded in black
The 11th stair transparent beyond a simple crack
The 12th stair a raft as blood rushes everywhere
The 13th stair collapses as if it wasn't meant to be there
Back to the beginning you go to climb the thirteen stairs

Death Labyrinth

For hours and hours you look around and roam
You just want to get out, you just want to go home
But this strange place has other plans
Out of the walls come faces and hands
Trying to grab you and take you within
They say to stay alive you must win
You keep making turns and jumping over hurdles
Only to feel that your going around in circles
Those that are in here are not your friends
Getting you lost leading you to dead ends
Around every corner something awaits
In order to escape you must do whatever it takes
An endless maze not in the slightest bit established
But a carnival like amusement they call it the Death Labyrinth

Resurrection

The night stands still
the moon goes to bed
They're coming out to kill, (who?)
the long awaited dead
Hands are coming out of the ground
the moment has finally arrived
not a trace of a single sound
the dead now become alive
a chant has been spoken
a spell has been cast
the dead have awoken
and they're out of their caskets
The day has finally come
They have made their selection
It's time for some fun
For the dead's resurrection

The Philosophy of Carnage

There is but a stillness inside every cerebral
Tiny waterfalls of blood vessels rushing, becoming lethal
Most overcome this trait some are less fortunate
Their minds not fully developed but dormant
In their unconscious minds a memory chip is inserted
To change things around till they're inverted
So now the mind is poisoned with a virus
One that calculates and stimulates with violence
Horror and terror take on whole new meanings
Turning nice people into bloodthirsty prototype beings
They know not of what they do nor do they care
Overtaken by darkness, emotions no longer there
They seize opportunities without even thinking
Corrupting the mind further and further into shrinking
Until its no longer active but taken hostage
The minds a terrible thing to waste with the philosophy of carnage

Inhibitors of Doom

Their agenda is simple, to make you live out your fears
To make you feel pain so bad you do more then shed tears
They take away your feelings and sense of reaction
The fact that your now unaware gives them satisfaction
You're a puppet now and they're pulling the strings
Having you do strange but innovative things
Creating chaos and putting your plans up in smoke
They want to see you fail they want to see you choke
It's like you had a lobotomy and they took out the frontal lobe
Making you into a wanderer, turning you into a probe
It's a little test they run to see how one takes being possessed
If you pass then in your services the devil will invest
Soon you will be one of them taken in by gloom
Just another spirit soldier, an inhibitor of doom

The Executioner

Only known for his everyday job
He acts professional and is not a slob
His identity is hidden by a black hood
To train for his job he practices chopping wood
He is called upon to bring forth vengeance
Has a cold heart and cares not for acceptance
Doesn't care if they're guilty or innocent
It's death not justice that he represents
His weapon of choice a sharp great axe
Used only for duty not for attacks
It's all in a days work getting hit with blood splatters
After all getting it done is all that really matters
Little known about a man so obscure
But I'm sure you would be too if you were and executioner

About the Author

Justin Bienvenue has been writing poetry for quite some time. It started off as something he liked to do to pass time but soon it became so much more. It has become a part of his life to which he enjoys very much and tries to write poems as often as he can.
"I have no specific topics, I write poems for just about anything." With no topic out of his range it is only a wonder as to what he may write about next.

Made in the USA
Middletown, DE
23 September 2017